Studies and documents on cultural policies

Recent titles in this series:

For a complete list of titles see page 52

Cultural policy in the

Byelorussian Soviet Socialist Republic

Institute of Art Criticism,
Ethnography and Folklore
of the Academy of Sciences
of the Byelorussian SSR

Unesco

Published in 1979 by the United Nations Educational,
Scientific and Cultural Organization,
7 Place de Fontenoy, 75700 Paris
Printed by Union Typographique, Villeneuve-Saint-Georges

ISBN 92-3-101579-6
*La Politique Culturelle dans
la République Socialiste Soviétique
de Biélorussie:* 92-3-201579-X

Preface

The purpose of this series is to show how cultural policies are planned and implemented in various Member States.

As cultures differ, so does the approach to them; it is for each Member State to determine its cultural policy and methods according to its own conception of culture, its socio-economic system, political ideology and technical development. However, the methods of cultural policy (like those of general development policy) have certain common problems; these are largely institutional, administrative and financial in nature, and the need has increasingly been stressed for exchanging experiences and information about them. This series, each issue of which follows as far as possible a similar pattern so as to make comparison easier, is mainly concerned with these technical aspects of cultural policy.

In general, the studies deal with the principles and methods of cultural policy, the evaluation of cultural needs, administrative structures and management, planning and financing, the organization of resources, legislation, budgeting, public and private institutions, cultural content in education, cultural autonomy and decentralization, the training of personnel, institutional infrastructures for meeting specific cultural needs, the safeguarding of the cultural heritage, institutions for the dissemination of the arts, international cultural co-operation and other related subjects.

The studies, which cover countries belonging to differing social and economic systems, geographical areas and levels of development, present, therefore, a wide variety of approaches and methods in cultural policy. Taken as a whole, they can provide guidelines to countries which have yet to establish cultural policies, while all countries, especially those seeking new formulations of such policies, can profit by the experience already gained.

This study was prepared for Unesco by the Institute of Art Criticism,

Ethnography and Folklore of the Academy of Sciences of the Byelorussian SSR.

The opinions expressed are the author's and do not necessarily reflect
the view of Unesco.

Contents

Contents

Introduction

Among the great objectives set for the building of communism in the Union of Soviet Socialist Republics, of which the Byelorussian SSR is a federated republic, great importance is attached to the continuous development of socialist culture. Communism is the conscious creation of history assumed by millions of people. Culture plays a vital role in the building of communism since, by its very essence, it stimulates creative activity and prepares man to engage in it.

For V. I. Lenin, the founder of the Soviet State, the immense significance of the Great October Socialist Revolution, the sixtieth anniversary of which was celebrated on 7 November 1977, lay in the fact that it led the broad working masses to embark on a course whereby they themselves shape history.

Lenin was the greater builder of the new socialist culture. Before the revolution, he established the principles and bases of the culture of the future socialist State, and subsequently did much to ensure the application, in practice, of the most important Marxist theses on this subject. From the very first days of the triumph of the October Revolution, he attached great importance to the development of culture in the Soviet Union, culture being regarded by him as one of the corner-stones on which the new workers' State was to be built.

In pointing out the ways by which the country of the Soviets could move forward towards socialism and communism, Lenin showed scientifically—and the experience of history has confirmed the correctness of his views—that one of the main factors in the building of a new society is a revolution in the cultural sphere, whereby all the accumulated wealth of human thought, and that still being created in the present, acquires fresh impetus and becomes the possession of the people as a whole. It is illuminated and inspired by the revolutionary, communist conception of the world, and serves to further the harmonious progress of society and the individual.

9

Introduction

Lenin ceaselessly emphasized that, in order to build socialism, it is absolutely vital to make provision, with the aid of the State, for rapid and scientifically based cultural progress to promote the development of popular culture in the broadest sense of the term. 'The harmonious development of man, spiritual and physical,' said L. I. Brezhnev, Secretary General of the Central Committee of the Communist Party of the Soviet Union (CPSU) and Chairman of the Presidium of the Supreme Soviet of the USSR, 'such, for Lenin, was the supreme significance of the revolution, socialism and communism.' [1]

Socialist society, having ensured the flowering of culture, national in form and socialist in content, is anxious to give all its members the opportunity to develop their creative faculties to the full by performing socially useful work. It stimulates the cultural evolution of man, both materially and morally, by leading him on to all-round spiritual development. Enormous resources are set aside each year in the State budget for education, the expansion of cultural facilities and the improvement of cultural services for the population. Under socialism, the Communist Party and the Soviet State pay as much attention to cultural as they do to economic development. It has become a tradition in our country to define State plans as plans for economic and cultural construction and, when reviewing the achievements of the people as a whole, to begin by emphasizing what has been done in these areas. The CPSU has prepared and is consistently implementing a scientifically based economic strategy for the attainment of certain fundamental, long-term goals, chief of which is to raise the material and cultural level of the people and to apply in practice the slogan of the Communist Party: 'Everything for man, everything for the good of man!'

The importance of cultural development is increasing at the present stage of the evolution of Soviet society, which is demanding ever greater spiritual qualities of workers. 'It is impossible to make progress in the important task of building communism without the all-round development of the individual,' stressed the Secretary General of the Committee of the CPSU and Chairman of the Presidium of the Supreme Soviet of the USSR, L. I. Brezhnev. 'Communism is impossible without an advanced level of culture, education, social consciousness and spiritual maturity, just as it is impossible in the absence of an adequate material and technical foundation.' [2]

The XXVth Congress of the CPSU, held in February-March 1976, devoted a great deal of attention to the problems of cultural development in the light of the very important tasks confronting society at the present stage of the building of advanced socialism. The policy of the Soviet

1. L. I. Brezhnev, *On the Path of Lenin. Speeches and Articles*, Vol. 4, p. 423, Moscow, 1974.
2. *Documents of the XXIVth Congress of CPSU*, p. 83, Moscow, 1971.

Communist Party is constantly to raise the material and cultural level of the people with a view to improving the material and technological basis of communism, perfecting social relations, forming a new type of man and developing a socialist way of life.

Principal stages
in the development of culture
in the Byelorussian SSR

The Byelorussian Soviet Socialist Republic is a socialist workers' and peasants' State which united, of its own free will, with the other republics of the Union of Soviet Socialist Republics, all equal in rights, to form a federate State. The highest organ of power in the Byelorussian SSR is the Supreme Soviet of the Byelorussian SSR and the highest executive body is the Council of Ministers.

The Byelorussian SSR covers an area of 207,600 square kilometres. At 1 January 1977, it had a population of 9,400,000. Its capital is the hero city of Minsk, which has 1,230,000 inhabitants.

Development of the Byelorussian SSR
since the October Revolution

Before the Great October Revolution, Byelorussia was a backward province of the Russian empire. Tsarism regarded it as a market for manufactured goods and a source of raw materials, and deliberately slowed down its industrial and agricultural development. The tsarist authorities kept the Byelorussian people in a state of ignorance and did everything to stifle all manifestations of their ancient national culture. Eighty per cent of the population were illiterate. There were no higher educational establishments; and the publication of books in the Byelorussian language was forbidden.

The Revolution liberated the Byelorussian people from social and national oppression, led them to embark on the conscious shaping of history and created conditions conducive to the development of the Byelorussian SSR.

The formation of the Byelorussian Soviet Socialist Republic on 1 January 1919 was a great event in the history of the Byelorussian people. It testified to the triumph of Marxism-Leninism and proletarian inter-

13

nationalism in our country, and was a magnificently successful application of the Leninist national policy followed by the Communist Party.

The victory of the Great October Socialist Revolution was a turning-point in the destiny of the Byelorussian peoples, and set the country on the path to social, economic and cultural progress. Under the direction of the Communist Party, the workers successfully accomplished the principal and highly complex task of the socialist revolution —that of creating the socialist State—and implemented Lenin's programme for the building of socialism, which covers all aspects of the life of society.

A very important step for the future of the Byelorussian people and the attainment of the objectives of socialism was the taking of the decision by the Byelorussian SSR, in December 1922, to unite of its own free will with the other Soviet republics to form the fraternal Union of Soviet Socialist Republics. The creation of the USSR was in accordance with the vital interests of all the peoples of our multinational mother-land, and acted as a powerful stimulus to the economic, political and cultural development of the Byelorussian SSR. Aided by all their Soviet brother peoples, the workers of the Byelorussian SSR quickly repaired the destruction caused by the world war, and the civil war, and the effects of foreign intervention, and set the national economy os its feet.

Through the implementation of Lenin's plan for industrialization and the collectivization of agriculture, Byelorussia was transformed, in the course of the first five-year plans, into a socialist republic with a flourishing industry and agriculture.

Simultaneously with the development of the socialist economy, much was done for the promotion of culture and science. The socialist cultural revolution produced remarkable results. Illiteracy was abolished. A dense network of schools, technical colleges, higher educational establishments, research institutes and cultural institutions was established throughout the territory of the Byelorussian SSR. Byelorussian Soviet personnel were trained in large numbers. The culture of the Byelorussian people, national in form and socialist in content, attained a high level.

Unhappily, the peaceful creative work of the Soviet people was interrupted by the perfidious attack launched against our country by fascist Germany in June 1941. The whole Soviet people rose in arms to defend their native land, and engaged in a fight to the death against fascism. More than a million Byelorussians fought side by side with all the Soviet brother peoples during the Great Patriotic War. From the first to the last day of the war, the flame of the partisan struggle never ceased to burn on Byelorussian territory, temporarily occupied by the enemy. In the partisan units, operating clandestinely, more than 440,000 fighters waged a self-sacrificing combat against the enemy. By defending the new political and social system, born of the October Revolution, and also their native Soviet land, the people of the Byelorussian SSR together

14

with all the other Soviet peoples confirmed their loyalty and unshakable devotion to the ideals of socialism.

The victory over fascism cost the people dear. Over 2,230,000 people, or one in every four inhabitants of the republic, lost their lives in the fight against the invaders. The Nazis left behind them a land looted, destroyed and scorched. They ruined over 10,000 factories, laid waste all the State and collective farms, destroyed over 80 per cent of urban dwellings, set fire to 9,200 villages, and looted and destroyed scientific, cultural and educational establishments. All in all the republic, during the war, lost over half its national wealth.

None the less, thanks to the heroic efforts of its workers and to the generous aid received from the other Soviet peoples, the Byelorussian SSR was able to surmount post-war difficulties, raise the towns and villages rapidly from the ruins and the ashes, build new factories and works, set up new State and collective farms and reorganize educational, scientific and cultural establishments. By 1950, the national economy was well on the way to being restored, and new construction work was being carried out with improved techniques. During the next twenty years, the Byelorussian SSR made constant progress in all domains. It developed its industries, mechanized its agriculture and attained a high level of cultural development.

During the period of the ninth five-year plan (1971-75), industrial production increased by 64 per cent, the overall production of the collective and State farms by 22 per cent and the national income by 47 per cent. At the present time, the monthly figure for industrial production is the same as for the whole of the year 1952.

During this ninth five-year plan, the main goal—the improvement of the well-being of the population—was untiringly pursued. To this end, the republic spent three times more than in the five preceding years. Real per-capita income increased approximately 1.3 times, the monthly salaries of workers and employees increased by 18.4 per cent and the incomes of collective farm workers by 37 per cent. The overall volume of the social consumption funds increased 1.4 times. These funds were used for raising the pensions of workers, employees, collective-farm workers, war wounded and victims of industrial accidents; for increasing assistance to the families of those killed fighting for their country, and paying larger grants to students attending specialized secondary and higher educational establishments; and for improving the situation of large families. The funds earmarked for the care and education of children likewise increased. Nearly 22 million square metres of dwelling space were built, and almost one in five of the republic's inhabitants have been provided with new living quarters.

Great progress has been made in science, culture, education and public health. More than 800 million roubles, or 1.5 times more than was spent during the eighth five-year plan, have been invested by the State

15

in developing those sectors and providing material facilities for them. Broadly general secondary education has now been made universal. The number of specialists graduating from establishments of higher education has increased by 46 per cent and of specialists completing courses at specialized secondary schools by 31 per cent. At the present time, more than 3.5 million inhabitants of the Byelorussian SSR, or one person in three, are receiving education of one kind or another. A total of 858,000 specialists with higher or specialized secondary education are employed in the republic's economy.

Considerable progress has been made in science. The Academy of Sciences of the Byelorussian SSR has over 180 research centres, employing 32,000 research workers and about 60,000 specialists, including 9,500 doctors and masters (candidates) of science, working in the sciences or in higher scientific education.

Some 200 newspapers and journals are published in the republic. During the ninth five-year plan, nearly 14,000 different books and pamphlets were published, the total number of copies being approximately 150 million.

Considerable success has likewise been achieved in the development of literature, music, the theatre and visual art. Speaking of the principal economic and social achievements of the ninth five-year plan, P. M. Masherov, alternate member of the Politburo of the Central Committee of the CPSU and First Secretary of the Central Committee of the Communist Party of the Byelorussian SSR, said in the report on the activity of the Central Committee, submitted to the XXVIIIth Congress of the Communist Party of the Byelorussian SSR:

At this stage of socialism, the development of the economy is more and more completely and fundamentally being directed towards the fuller satisfaction of man's material and spiritual needs. This was the main objective of the ninth five-year plan, and such will continue to be the objective of the Party's economic and social policy in the future. [1]

New horizons are today opening up before the Byelorussian SSR as a result of the tenth five-year plan (1976-80). The main objective of this plan is consistently to apply the policy of the Communist Party for improving the material and cultural standard of living of the people through developing social production and making it more efficient, accelerating technical and scientific progress and improving the productivity and quality of work in all sectors of the national economy.

The law on the State Five-year Plan for Promoting the Development of the National Economy of the Byelorussian SSR in 1976-80, adopted

1. *Documents of hte XXVIIIth Congress of the Communist Party of the Byelorussian SSR*, p. 12, Minsk, 1976.

by the Supreme Soviet of the republic, states that industrial production is to be increased by 43 per cent in relation to the previous five-year period, mean annual agricultural production by 12 per cent and the national income of the republic by 34 per cent.

With a view to the implementation of the programme adopted by the XXVth Congress of the CPSU for the social development and the constant improvement of the material and cultural level of the population, this law provides for the following measures:

Real per-capita income is to be increased by 21.5 per cent.

The average wage of workers and employees is to be increased by approximately 22 per cent and the wages of collective farm workers are to be increased by an average of 32 per cent by improving output and the quality of work.

Grants and benefits received by the population from the social consumption funds are to be increased by approximately 30 per cent.

A total of 22.5 million square metres of living accommodation is to be provided for the population.

It is also intended to increase the number of children attending pre-school establishments by 29.9 per cent and the number attending technical vocational establishments by 11 per cent. At the same time, the number of students attending specialized secondary schools is to be increased by 8.3 per cent and the number of those attending establishments of higher education by 5.6 per cent.

Measures are likewise to be taken to ensure the continuous development of science, which has become an important factor of progress. The material and technical infrastructure is to be strengthened, the network of scientific research institutions is to be extended and scientific establishments are to be created capable of developing ideas from their conception to their practical application.

Measures will also be taken regarding the press, television and radio. The material and technical equipment of cultural establishments will be improved, particularly in country districts. New cinemas, clubs and cultural centres will be built, and the library network will be extended.

Main stages of the cultural revolution

In the course of the great economic and social changes our country has undergone, the Communist Party and the Soviet State have been successful in solving the problems posed by the cultural revolution, which is an integral part of the Leninist plan for the building of socialism.[1] According to Lenin, the cultural revolution rests on three essential premises: the

---

1. See, in this connection, A. A. Zvorykin *et al., Cultural Policy in the Union of Soviet Socialist Republics,* Paris, Unesco, 1970.

first is to have a completely literate population and to develop public education; the second, to train highly qualified personnel recruited from the ranks of workers and peasants, for all branches of the national economy; the third, to change the outlook of the people, so that they understand the basis of the new economic and social regime and see the need for building socialism and communism.

Since its beginnings, the socialist cultural revolution has passed through a number of stages, corresponding to the stages in the development of the economic bases which, in the context of socialism, govern all social relations.

The first stage in the cultural revolution in our country was the period from the Great October Socialist Revolution to the mid-1930s. At this time, the principal task was to inculcate a socialist attitude in the population, reinforce and develop the ideological and theoretical bases of the working class, give the peasants a Soviet outlook on life and a collective spirit, and form a new socialist intelligentsia composed of workers and peasants. The new culture, national in form and socialist in content, developed initially by drawing on the national traditions and cultural heritage of the people.

The second stage in the cultural revolution extended from the end of the 1930s to the 1950s. During this stage, the building of socialism in our country was completed and socialist ideology triumphed and was firmly implanted in all of intellectual life: science, social philosophy, literature, art and ethics. New national leaders in science and culture, trained in the spirit of Marxism-Leninism, brought a fresh interpretation to the cultural heritage of the peoples they represented, and drew great inspiration from national traditions in order to ensure the continuous development of a new type of culture, national in form and socialist in content.

During the present period of the history of the Soviet State, now that socialist culture has triumphed and is steadily expanding, our country has reached the final stage of the socialist cultural revolution, the stage of the creation of the conditions necessary for the transition from socialism to communism. This final stage of the cultural revolution corresponds to the stage of advanced socialism which has been set up in our country.

Advanced socialism is a normal stage of the evolution towards communism. At this stage, socialism, developing on its own basis, manifests more completely its creative potentialities and its profound humanism. Advanced socialism is characterized by a combination of the progress resulting from the scientific and technological revolution and the advantages of the socialist system. It represents a step towards the rapid intensification of the development of the economy, the increase of production and the solution of the problems raised by the creation of the material and technical foundation of communism, and it ensures the

18

continuous improvement of the material and cultural level of the people. Advanced socialism illustrates the extreme maturity of the whole system of social relations, gradually being transformed into communist relations.

At the stage of advanced socialism, socialist culture is a powerful factor in the development of the whole of social life. It contributes to the harmonious development of the workers and to the manifestation of their creative capacities, to the growth of their social needs and to the application of the people's creative energy to the establishment of new and higher forms of community life. As culture develops, the Soviet way of life becomes more highly perfected, demonstrating that the great achievements of socialism have become an integral part of our life.

Socialist culture owes to Marxism-Leninism, which constitutes its kernel and is itself the fruit of the evolution of human culture, all the successes it is achieving in its ascent to ever loftier summits. 'Marxism has acquired its historic significance as the ideology of the revolutionary proletariat', wrote Lenin, 'because far from rejecting the most valuable achievements of the bourgeois epoch, it has, on the contrary, assimilated and refashioned everything of value in the more than two thousand years of the development of human thought and culture.' [1]

Marxism-Leninism has, in its turn, stimulated the development of the finest traditions and most valuable achievements of the existing culture and has created the conditions necessary for the formation and evolution of a new socialist culture by combining all the specific traits and rich traditions of the national culture of each of the fraternal peoples of the Soviet Union.

Socialist culture has become one of the factors essential to the establishment of advanced socialism. Hence the main objective of the great economic and social development programme for Soviet society, drawn up by the XXVth Congress of the CPSU, is 'the constant growth of the part played by culture in the ideological, political, moral and aesthetic education of the Soviet people, and in the development of their spiritual needs.' [2]

The main features of the development of culture are as follows: continuous development of education in accordance with the requirements of scientific and technological progress, so as constantly to raise the technological, cultural and educational levels of the workers, and to improve the training of skilled personnel; development of the study of the laws of nature and society; strengthening of the contribution made by science to the solution of the vital problems attendant on the construction of the material and technical foundation of communism; the acceleration of scientific and technical progress; higher efficiency in production; increased well-being and a higher cultural level for the people; the intro-

1. V. I. Lenin, *Collected Works*, Vol. 31, p. 317 (English edition).
2. *Documents of the XXVth Congress of the CPSU*, p 221, Moscow, 1976.

duction of workers to the conception of the communist world; the regular development of all the arts; improvement and development of the material facilities of educational, scientific and cultural establishments; improvement in the activity of cultural institutions; extension of the network of libraries and clubs; improvement of the work of people's universities and museums, and of the measures undertaken for the protection of historical and cultural monuments; and the steady development of publishing, radio, television and cinema.

Establishment and improvement of the State system for the organization of culture

Radical changes have been made in all areas of social life thanks to the triumph of the Great October Socialist Revolution, which gave the workers unprecedented opportunities for developing their creative faculties. By replacing private ownership of the means of production by collective ownership, the Revolution gave the working people all the material resources necessary for the development of culture. After conferring power on the workers, it radically changed the content and functions of culture, which henceforth became the culture of the people. The October Revolution made the revolutionary ideology of the proletariat—Marxism-Leninism—the ideological basis for the development of a new type of culture.

The establishment and improvement of the State management of culture has been a constant feature of the development of Soviet Byelorussia.

Directly after the founding of the Byelorussian SSR, in the difficult conditions resulting from the destruction wrought by the world war and foreign intervention, the Soviet authorities began to investigate the problem of the most efficient forms of cultural action. January 1919 saw the establishment of the People's Commissariat for Education, which was made responsible for education and culture. The literacy campaign called for an immense effort by the people and the State. Work was begun on opening schools, culture and art establishments, theatres, libraries, clubs, rural reading rooms and other institutions which played an important part in introducing the people to culture. Clubs for amateur cultural activities were opened in large numbers.

The resolution adopted by the Vth Congress of the Communist Party of the Byelorussian SSR (October 1921), entitled 'Public Education and the Tasks of the Party', stated that 'Cultural activities in all fields should be based on the principle that these cannot be dissociated either from economic development or from the general policy of communism.'[1]

1. *Resolutions of the Congresses and Plenary Sessions of the Central Committee of the Communist Party of the Byelorussian SSR*, vol. 1, p. 71-2 (Russian text) Minsk, 1973.

20

Cultural activity, covering the instruction and training of the population in the spirit of communism, was considered to be the principal function of all establishments and bodies concerned with education, science, literature and art. The congress proclaimed the immutable nature of the State monopoly of all cultural establishments, and stressed the need for associating the broadest possible sections of the workers with the development of culture.

The Byelorussian State University, founded in 1921, played an important part in the training of national personnel, the study and development of culture and the creation of the right conditions for the founding of the Byelorussian Academy of Sciences, the Byelorussian Lenin State Library and various research and cultural institutions as well.

In 1922, the People's Commissariat for Education of the Byelorussian SSR set up the Institute of Byelorussian Culture, which undertook an enormous amount of scientific research in the field of linguistics, art criticism, literature, ethnography, history, economics and natural history. In 1926, this institute separated from the commissariat and became an independent academic establishment which, in 1928, was reorganized and named the Byelorussian Academy of Sciences (now the Academy of Sciences of the Byelorussian SSR). The government made the academy responsible for the methodological organization of all the scientific activities of the republic.

The year 1925 saw the creation of the Gorky Academy of Agriculture, on the basis of the institutes set up earlier at Minsk and Gorky.

In August 1920, the People's Commissariat for Education founded, in Minsk, the Byelorussian State Theatre (now the Y. Kupala Byelorussian State Theatre), and 1926 marked the creation of the Byelorussian Travelling Theatre, which in 1932 became the third Byelorussian State Theatre of Dramatic Art.

A Decree on the People's Commissariat for Education, approved at the end of 1924, made the commissariat responsible for the general organization of education, and of all institutes and bodies in the Byelorussian SSR concerned with education, culture, science and art. Sections with powers for carrying out the necessary work were established in the commissariat.

In December 1924, a special cinematography department was set up in the commissariat, to be responsible for the showing of films throughout the republic.

In 1933, the commissariat was reorganized into four departments, to cover the following fields: primary and secondary teaching; teacher training; library science; theatres; and nine sections, to be responsible for: pre-school education; kindergartens; teaching materials; adult schools and courses; reading-rooms, clubs, cultural centres, recreation parks; building, etc.

In the mid-1930s, the system of administration had to be changed as a result of the extension of the network of cultural establishments and

21

bodies. In 1936, a department of arts was established under the authority of the Government of the Byelorussian SSR, to take charge of theatres and other public halls, cinemas, academies of music, painting, sculpture, etc., including establishments providing training in drama, films, music and visual arts, formerly under the control of the People's Commissariat for Education. Libraries, cultural centres and reading rooms remained the responsibility of the commissariat until 1945 when they were transferred to the Committee for Cultural Establishments, set up under the Council of People's Commissars of the Byelorussian SSR. Sections responsible for cultural activities were set up in the regions and towns as part of the executive committee of the Soviets of workers' deputies. In the district executive committees, inspectors were appointed to supervise these activities.

In May 1953, with a view to centralizing the organization of cultural development, a Ministry of Culture for the Byelorussian SSR was established. This ministry comprised: a films department, responsible for film production; an arts department; a department for cultural establishments (with sections for clubs, parks, zoos, libraries, museums, historical and archeological monuments); a department for publishing and the book industry; a department for vocational training reorganized in 1955 to form the Republican Department for manpower reserves); a department for the book trade; a broadcasting department, and others.

About 1965, the functions and structure of the Ministry of Culture of the Byelorussian SSR were made more precise. At present, this ministry is responsible for drama and music, cultural activities, museums, the protection of historic and artistic monuments, the management of amateur cultural activities as regards their methods and the training of skilled personnel for cultural and art establishments.

Until 1959, higher and specialized secondary education came under the Ministry of Education of the Byelorussian SSR, but in 1959 the Ministry of Higher, Specialist Secondary and Vocational Education was set up to ensure further development in these fields. In 1966, the State Committee of the Council of Ministers of the Byelorussian SSR took over responsibility for vocational training from this ministry.

The State Committee of the Council of Ministers of the Byelorussian SSR is in charge of the production and showing of films in the republic, and of the training of film workers.

Responsibility for publishing, the book industry and book trade lies with the appropriate State Committee of the Council of Ministers of the Byelorussian SSR, which was set up in 1963.

In 1932, responsibility for broadcasting which had, until then, been vested in communications organizations, passed to the Broadcasting Committee, a body specially created for this purpose. In 1950, this committee was reorganized to become the Committee of Radio Information. In 1957, the State Committee for Television and Sound Broadcasting was created, attached to the Byelorussian SSR Council of Ministers.

The Republic's information organization is the Byelorussian SSR Telegraph Agency (BELTA) attached to the Council of Ministers of the republic.

On 14 April 1978, the Supreme Soviet of the Byelorussian Soviet Socialist Republic adopted the text of a new constitution which gives a solid basis for the subsequent development of the Republic in the socio-economic and cultural fields.

Education and the scientific study of cultural problems

Education

The Soviet State has created extremely favourable conditions for education and is making great efforts to provide education for the young generations. The goal of education in our country is to train men and women to build the communist society, highly cultivated people devoted to Marxist-Leninist ideas, imbued with respect for Soviet laws and the socialist legal order, with a communist attitude towards work, physically sound and capable of working effectively in the economic, social and cultural fields, and in particular of making an active contribution towards society and the State. Education is designed to guide the development of the spiritual and intellectual needs of Soviet people and, at the same time, to satisfy these needs.

In recent years, the Central Committee of the CPSU and the USSR Council of Ministers have drawn up a programme for the promotion of education, and special measures have been taken to develop and perfect general education, vocational training and specialized secondary and higher education. The aim of this is to ensure that the educational system as a whole meets the requirements of scientific and technological progress and corresponds to the goal of building communism, and to guarantee that education ties in more closely with the ideological and moral training of the young. In 1973, the Supreme Soviet of the USSR adopted the Bases of the Legislation of the USSR and of the Federal Republics on Public Education.

The Constitution of the Byelorussian SSR states that all citizens of the country have the right to education. This right is guaranteed by universal compulsory secondary education, vocational education ,and specialized secondary and higher education, all designed to prepare people for life and for the building of communism. The right to education is guaranteed by the fact that teaching is given in the pupil's mother tongue,

The Forest popular dance troupe from the Cultural Centre at Pinsk.

Musical week for the children and young people of all the republics of the Soviet Union, Minsk, 1976.

The Khatyn memorial.

Day of Byelorussian literature and art: closing concert.

Byelorussian State Academic Theatre for Opera and Ballet (Bolshoi Theatre) decorated with the Order of Lenin.

The Palace of Culture of the Orlovsky Aurore kolkhoz, Kirov district, Mogilev region.

Participants in the day of Ukrainian literature and art in the Byelorussian SSR in front of the statue of Lenin.

International Friendship Club, School No. 122 at Minsk.

by the existence of a large network of pre-school and out-of-school establishments, by the provision of all types of education free of charge, by the giving of State grants and other financial aids to students, and by the establishment of a system of polytechnical education designed to provide further training for workers. In addition, school and university students receive various other forms of aid under the law.

According to the Law on Public Education adopted by the Supreme Soviet of the Byelorussian SSR in December 1974, the main principles on which education is based are the following:

1. All citizens of the USSR have an equal right to education, without distinction of race, nationality, sex, attitude to religion or financial and social situation.
2. Education is compulsory for all children.
3. All educational and cultural establishments belong to society and to the State.
4. The language of instruction may be freely chosen (mother tongue or language of another of the peoples of the USSR).
5. Education is free of charge at all levels; the State pays for the maintenance of a proportion of the children; school pupils and students receive grants and other kinds of material assistance.
6. All educational establishments form part of a general system, comprising successive levels of instruction.
7. The school, the family and society all contribute towards the education of children and young people.
8. Education is kept closely linked to life and to practical work for the building of communism.
9. Education is scientific in character, and everything is done to adjust it continually to the latest advances in science, technology and culture.
10. Instruction and education are humanist and moral in character.
11. Education is mixed.
12. Education is non-religious.

The education system in the Byelorussian SSR comprises pre-school and primary education, general secondary education (including out-of-school education), vocational training, specialized secondary education and higher education.

GENERAL SECONDARY EDUCATION

Education for young people throughout the republic is provided through a secondary education system which constitutes an important feature of the economic, social and economic development of our society, engaged in the building of communism, and is designed to make the workers more socially conscious and to raise their cultural level.

The main objectives of general secondary education are as follows:
To give young people a secondary education corresponding to the present

needs of social, technological and scientific progress, provide them
with a sound knowledge of the fundamental sciences, and inspire
them with the desire to go on improving and adding to their
knowledge and to apply it in practice.

To inculcate in the young a Marxist-Leninist attitude to the world, a spirit
of socialist internationalism and Soviet patriotism.

To give young people a civic training corresponding to the moral code of
the builder of communism.

To ensure the pupils' harmonious development and general culture, to
give them aesthetic and physical training, and build up their health.

To prepare pupils to do socially useful work and to make an informed
choice of career.

General secondary education and pre- and out-of-school education come
under the Ministry of Education of the Byelorussian SSR, which is also
a Union Republican Ministry. It is responsible for the administration of
the teaching and educational establishments directly subordinate to it
and, through the appropriate administrative departments, co-ordinates
the activities of general education schools and pre-school and out-of-school
establishments. The ministry is also responsible for the training of
teachers and the development of the science of education.

In addition to the primary schools, the eight-year schools and the ten-
year general secondary schools, there are also a number of specialist
schools, e.g. schools where the teaching centres round certain subjects,
schools where certain subjects are taught in a foreign language, schools
specializing in the teaching of music, art or sport; sanatorium schools
located in forests, and young workers' evening schools which students
attend in their free time. In 1976, there were in the republic 8,400 general
education establishments with a total of 1.7 million pupils.

Thanks to the social, economic, technological and intellectual progress
made by the advanced socialist society, the transfer to general secondary
education has been largely achieved. The stage reached in this field can
be indicated by the following percentages: in 1965, 36.4 per cent of
young people had received a secondary education, while in 1970 the
figure was 76 per cent and, in 1975, 95 per cent. Using recent findings
in the science of education and the results of scientific, technological and
social progress, Soviet schools provide the knowledge required to enable
individuals and society as a whole to engage in creative activity.

There also exists in the Byelorussian SSR a vast network of para-
educational establishments such as pioneer centres and halls, centres for
young technicians, naturalists, hikers, etc., and childrens's libraries
(numbering more than 520 in 1976), all designed to promote the abilities
and special gifts of the young, arouse their interest in life in society,
work, science, technology, art and sport, and encourage them to organize
their leisure occupations and to build up their stamina. Para-educational
establishments organize the work of groups, associations, clubs etc.

where children are able to give free rein to their creative inclinations.

Teachers for general secondary schools are trained at colleges of education; primary and nursery school teachers are trained in secondary schools providing specialized pedagogical training.

The Ministry of Education of the republic employs a total of 130,000 people in the various educational departments and establishments.

VOCATIONAL EDUCATION

The objectives of vocational education are:

To train, for the national economy, skilled workers with a good general education and a high professional standard, able to meet the demands of modern production and scientific and technological progress and capable of ensuring their development.

To provide, in the technical vocational schools, both vocational training and general secondary education.

To inculcate in pupils a Marxist-Leninist outlook on the world, develop their moral qualities, train them in the spirit of socialist international-ism and Soviet patriotism, bring them to adopt a communist attitude towards work and collective ownership, and teach them to be always ready to defend and uphold the revolutionary and labour traditions of the working class.

To ensure pupils' aesthetic and physical education, and improve their health.

For admission to vocational training establishments, students are required to have completed the course at an eight-year school or a general secondary school.

Vocational training is governed by the State Committee for vocational training of the Byelorussian Council of Ministers. This controls the establishments and bodies directly subordinate to it, and supervises the standard of training given to skilled workers in vocational training establishments.

This type of training has been expanded in recent years. During the ninth five-year plan, the number of vocational schools has been increased fourfold, and the number of students by more than six times. Between 1971 and 1975, more than 320,000 specialists were trained in these establishments. In 1976, there were 188 vocational schools in the Byelorussian SSR, attended by 124,000 students.

SPECIALIZED SECONDARY EDUCATION

The purpose of this type of education is:

To train skilled personnel of a middle-level general and specialist standard, with a sound theoretical grounding and good professional skills, holding Marxist-Leninist ideas and capable of organizing political and educational activities for the masses.

To provide further training for specialists bearing in mind the requirements of modern production, science, technology and culture and
their probable development.

To inculcate high moral standards in students, promote a communist
attitude towards work and collective ownership, develop the spirit of
socialist internationalism and Soviet patriotism, and improve the
physical condition of the young.

Specialized secondary education establishments (technical colleges,
schools) admit students who have completed the course at the eight-year
or ten-year school.

Specialized secondary education comes under the Ministry of Specialist
Secondary and Higher Education of the Byelorussian SSR.

In 1976, there were 133 specialized secondary schools in the Byelorussian SSR, attended by 159,000 students and providing for 185 occupations.

HIGHER EDUCATION

Higher education is provided in universities, institutes and academies.
The main tasks of higher educational establishments are as follows:

To train highly qualified specialists and give them a sound knowledge of
Marxist-Leninist theory, a thorough grasp of the theoretical basis and
practical skills of their speciality and the ability to organize mass
political and educational activities.

To develop in students high moral principles, a communist outlook, a
spirit of socialist internationalism and Soviet patriotism, and to
improve their physical fitness.

To effect constant improvements in specialist training, bearing in mind
the demands of modern production, science, technology and culture
and the prospects for their development.

To carry out research work conducive to raising the standard of specialist
training and bringing about social, scientific and technological
progress.

To prepare textbooks and teaching materials.

To train qualified scientific personnel and teachers.

To provide further training for the teaching staff of specialized secondary
teaching establishments, and for specialists having had higher education working in the relevant branches of the national economy.

Establishments of higher education admit those who have completed
their secondary-level studies.

The Ministry of Specialist Secondary and Higher Education of the
Byelorussian SSR exercises direct control over higher and specialized
secondary educational establishments, institutions and organizations subordinate to it, is responsible, through the appropriate departments and
offices, for the methodological work of the other higher specialized

colleges, and supervises the teaching work of establishments of higher education and specialized secondary teaching establishments.

In 1976, there were two universities in the Byelorussian SSR, 28 institutes, and an academy of agriculture, training specialists for nearly 190 occupations. They had 165,000 students, and a teaching staff of 11,500, including nearly 5,000 doctors and masters (candidates) of science.

In the higher educational system of the Byelorussian SSR, an important part is played by those establishments which train qualified personnel for work in culture and the arts. Those intending to take up such employment attend the Lenin State University of the Byelorussian SSR and various other higher educational establishments.

The Byelorussian State Academy of Music, set up in 1932, is now an important centre for training pianists and players of wind, string and Byelorussian folk instruments, and for training singers, musicologists, composers, and choral, orchestral and symphonic conductors. The Academy of Music has a post-graduate study section, an opera studio, a specialized music school and a correspondence study section.

The faculty of music of the A. M. Gorky Institute of Education in Minsk also trains highly qualified music and singing teacher for general schools.

Founded in Minsk in 1946, the Theatre and Arts Institute now trains stage and film actors, theatrical producers, painters, sculptors, draughtsmen, specialists in the applied, monumental and decorative arts, and theatre and art critics.

Architects are trained at the Byelorussian State Polytechnic Institute and at the Institute of Civil Engineering at Brest.

The Byelorussian State Institute of Physical Culture, opened in Minsk in 1937, provides training for physical education teachers and instructors.

The inauguration, in 1975, of the Minsk Institute of Culture, a teaching and research centre which trains qualified staff to work in cultural establishments, was an important event in the cultural life of the republic.

Scientific study of cultural problems

In the Byelorussian SSR there are a number of specialized research centres actively engaged in the study of problems connected with culture and its history. They are as follows: Institute of Art Criticism, Ethnography and Folklore; Y. Kupala Institute of Literature; Y. Kolas Institute of Linguistics; Institute of Philosophy and of Law; Institute of History; and Institute of Economics. Cultural problems are also studied at the Byelorussian State University, the Byelorussian State Academy of Music, the Byelorussian Institute of Theatre and Art, the Byelorussian State Polytechnical Institute, the Minsk Institute of Culture, the Gomel State University, the Minsk Institute of Education, the Brest Institute of Civil Engineering, and various other higher educational establishments.

The research institutes of the Byelorussian SSR Academy of Sciences co-ordinate all research work on the history and theory of culture. Certain theoretical and practical problems of culture, concerning the present development of folk art and crafts, are also studied by the various unions of creative workers which have literary and art criticism sections. The Union of Composers has a folklore section.

Republican and All Union publishing houses have brought out a large number of general theoretical works on music, drama and television and a considerable number of monographs on the history of certain special forms of modern Byelorussian art and on the philosophy of art in the Byelorussian SSR.

Important work is being done on the history and theory of Byelorussian literature. Collections of Byelorussian literary classics—by Y. Kupala, Y. Kolas, M. Bogdanovich, K. Cherny, etc.—are published regularly and also the works of contemporary writers such as P. Brovka, M. Tank, M. Lynkov, K. Krapiva, A. Kuliashov, I. Mélezh, I. Shamyakin. V. Bykov, P. Panchenka and others. The Academy of Sciences of the Byelorussian SSR is now bringing out a collection of folklore in several volumes, containing the best examples of Byelorussian folk poetry.

The year 1975 marked the completion of the publication of the *Byelorussian Soviet Encyclopedia,* comprising twelve volumes and covering all the principal fields of knowledge. Copies of this monumental work were presented to the libraries of the United Nations in New York, the United Nations Office in Geneva and Unesco in Paris.

The *Corpus of the Monuments of Byelorussian History and Culture* is now in the course of preparation. This 'Corpus' will indicate the place and role of the cultural heritage of the Byelorussian people in the history of the peoples of the USSR and the culture of the world, and will serve as a basis on which to organize activities for the protection of historical, architectural and archaeological monuments.

Artistic culture and means of cultural communication

The development of culture is ensured by All Union State and social bodies and by republican organizations. This makes it possible to allow for the specific features of each of the federal republics, while safeguarding the development of culture of the Soviet Union as a whole.

Unions of creative workers

Writers, painters, sculptors, composers, film workers, dramatists, television workers, the staff of cultural establishments, journalists and critics, all have their own voluntary social organizations—the unions of creative workers. The purpose of these unions is to promote the development of literature and the arts, to raise the ideological and professional standard of their members, and to create the conditions necessary for the expression of talent. Each of these unions is directed by its congress which meets every four or five years; its executive organ is the administrative council. In 1976, the Byelorussian Union of Writers had 304 members; the Union of Painters, 402; the Union of Architects, 550; the Union of Film Workers, 144; the Union of Journalists, 2,100; the Union of Composers, 48; and the Byelorussian Theatre Association, 1,422. All in all, the creative unions of the Byelorussian Republic have a membership of about 5,000.

The unions of creative workers have their own budgets and their own resources deriving from members' subscriptions and other cash income. For example, the Union of Writers and the Union of Composers receive statutory levies from the takings at events such as concerts, literary evenings, etc., and from the income of publishing houses. The Union of Film Workers, in addition to its members' subscriptions, possesses funds deriving from the various activities of its Soviet film publicity section (books, lectures, concerts). The Union of Painters derives its

31

income from orders carried out by its workshops and groups, and also from exhibitions. The Union of Architects collects dues from architects' offices.

The Byelorussian SSR Union of Writers is affiliated to the Union of Writers of the USSR. The history of its development is parallel to that of socialist realist literature. The 1920s saw the emergence in the Byelorussian SSR of a number of literary and art associations such as 'Youth', 'Summits', 'The Literary and Art Association', and 'The Byelorussian Association of Proletarian Writers'. In the early 1930s the need arose to combine these separate organizations in a single union of creative workers. The first Byelorussian Congress of Writers, held in 1934, established the Union of Writers of the Byelorussian SSR, which now comprises seven sections (prose, poetry, theatre, cinema, criticism, children's books and library translations). There are committees dealing with patriotic literature, links with other republics of the USSR and with foreign countries, and co-operation with young authors. The union has branches in Grodno, Mogilev and Gomel.

The Union of Composers of the Byelorussian SSR fosters the development of Byelorussian music and helps musical groups and performers to plan their programme. It has sections dealing with musical criticism, folk music, light music and music for children.

The Union of Architects provides effective aid to social and State bodies in the planning and construction of towns, districts, cultural premises for industrial, agricultural and public services, and blocks of dwellings. Its purpose is to strengthen collaboration between architects, painters and builders, and to develop the means of artistic expression. It thus fulfils an immensely important ideological, aesthetic and educational role. Within this union are committees dealing with town planning, the architecture of public buildings, industrial architecture, rural architecture, townscapes, the synthesis of arts and architecture, new building materials, the architecture of commercial and common services buildings, the training of architects, the architecture of schools and pre-school establishments, the architectural heritage and modern architecture. Byelorussian architects play an active part in the rebuilding of towns and villages bearing in mind the new demands now made on architecture.

Membership of the Union of Painters of the Byelorussian SSR is open to artists of all kinds and to art critics. It has sections dealing with painting, graphic art, sculpture, stage designing, films and television, decorative art, monumental art, art criticism, posters, etc. The union also has committees responsible for publicity about visual art, the organization of exhibitions, and co-operation with amateur artists.

In addition, the union organizes regular exhibitions at the Fine Arts Museum, in its own arts centre and also in the exhibition halls of regional centres, towns and districts. A Visual Arts Week, held once a year, helps to familiarize the public with the work of painters and engravers.

The Union of Journalists of the Byelorussian SSR exists for journalists working on periodicals, in television, radio, and news agencies and publishing houses.

The Union of Film Workers caters for scenario-writers and film directors, cameramen, painters, actors and critics. It has sections specializing in art films, documentaries, popular-science films, television, film criticism, cinema equipment and amateur film-making.

The Byelorussian Theatrical Society caters for producers, actors, painters, stage-designers, musicians, critics, translators, librettists and theatre specialists. It has sections specializing in theatre criticism, production, opera and amateur theatricals.

The unions of creative workers are anxious both to reinforce the ideological training of their members and to assist them in perfecting their professional skills. To this end, they organize regular conferences and seminars for young writers, composers, painters and film workers, whose work they examine with the assistance of artists of repute. The unions also organize competitions, exhibitions and public concerts.

These unions have publicity offices responsible for organizing lectures and gatherings at which writers, composers, painters, theatre and cinema personalities and architects meet the public. They also arrange for artists and performers to be interviewed on television and radio.

The Byelorussian creative workers' unions maintain close contacts with writers and artists in all the other federal republics of the USSR, with the socialist countries and with progressive representatives of culture in the various countries of the world. These unions arrange missions, exchanges of exhibitions, concerts, theatrical and other performances, co-productions of films, and discussions on the problems of the development of literature and the arts, all of which enable creative artists to make progress in their particular field.

The unions use their funds to provide their members with material and financial aid in their artistic activities and research and publicity work. They send their members on missions to towns and villages so that they can see the major focuses of activity in the country. They have their own creative work and rest centres.

As a token of recognition by society and the State of the value of their work, awards are made to the most eminent artists of prizes (Lenin prize, the USSR and Byelorussian State prizes, Leninist Komsomol prizes and prizes of the Republican Komsomol Organization); titles (hero of socialist work, people's artist of the USSR, people's painter of the USSR, people's architect of the USSR, honoured artist and people's artist of the Byelorussian SSR, national writer and national poet of the Byelorussian SSR, people's painter of the Byelorussian SSR, outstanding artistic figure of the Byelorussian SSR and outstanding cultural worker of the Byelorussian SSR); and decorations (orders and medals of the Soviet Union). Numerous creative workers of the republic have received titles and orders from other federal republics of the USSR, and have received titles and awards at national and international festivals and competitions, as well as orders and medals from the community of socialist countries.

Theatres and musical establishments

The Byelorussian SSR has fourteen professional theatres which include eight drama theatres, one opera and ballet theatre, one lyric theatre, one young people's theatre and three puppet theatres. In addition, the capital of the republic is the headquarters of the Byelorussian State Philharmonic, the State Symphony Orchestra, the Popular Instrumental Ensemble, the Chamber Orchestra, the Academic Choir, the National Choir of the Byelorussian SSR, and the Byelorussian Song and Dance Ensemble.

The theatres and artistic groups of the Byelorussian SSR stage some 20,000 shows and concerts annually, attended by over 6 million people.

The theatres put on successful productions of Russian and Byelorussian classics, as well as works of contemporary authors, both Soviet and foreign.

The repertoire of the theatres is planned with a view to inculcating a spirit of humanism and justice. The theatre and concert halls ban works calculated to incite cruelty, violence, pornography and the dehumanization of man. During the past few years, Byelorussian theatres and concert halls have presented productions which have been very much appreciated by the public. These have included the operas *Mindia* by Taktakishvili and *Don Juan* by Mozart; the ballets *Carmen Suite* by Bizet/Schedrin, *Alpine Ballad* by Glebov, *The Dream* and *Till Eulenspiegel*, presented in the Byelorussian Opera and Ballet Theatre; the plays *The Ravaged Nest* by Kupala, *The Tribunal* by Makaenok, *The Men on the Marsh* by Melezh, *Characters* by Shukshin—produced by the Y. Kupala Academic Theatre of the Byelorussian SSR; *Macbeth* by Shakespeare, *Vassili Terkin* by Tvardovski, *The Final Authority* by Matukovski, presented by the M. Gorky Russian Drama Theatre of the Byelorussian SSR. The Young People's Theatre presented *The Examination in Autumn* by Shamyakin, and *Four Drops* by Rosov; and the Y. Kolas Drama Theatre presented *The Pill under the Tongue* by Makaenok and *Energetic People* by Shukshin.

The theatre companies and artistic groups of the republic tour widely. At the same time, theatre companies from various towns in the Soviet Union visit the Republic regularly. Companies from Moscow, Leningrad, Kiev, Lvov, Zaporozhye and other cities were in the Byelorussia SSR recently.

Professional troupes strive hard to satisfy the cultural needs of the population. For many years past, the State Philharmonic has given concerts of symphonic and chamber music on a subscription basis. It aims to familiarize the public with Russian and foreign classical music as well as the music of Byelorussian composers. Since 1974, several philharmonic orchestras of the republic have taken part every year in a musical festival known as 'Byelorussian Musical Autumn'.

Museums

There are 52 State museums in the Byelorussian SSR, with 11 branch museums. In addition there are, in schools, cultural centres and clubs, more than 600 museums organized on a voluntary basis.

The largest museum in the Republic is the Byelorussian State Museum of the History of the Great Patriotic War where objects are exhibited that illustrate the exploits of the Soviet people during the war. There is also a war museum in the memorial Hero-fortress of Brest, and a museum of Soviet-Polish military co-operation has been opened in the village of Lenino (Gorky district, region of Mogilev).

The historical Museum of the Byelorussian SSR recounts the history of the Byelorussian people.

The State Museum of Fine Arts contains paintings, drawings and sculptures by artists of the nineteenth and early twentieth centuries, and also works by contemporary Byelorussian artists.

All museums take active measures to interest the general public in their collections. During the past few years, a number of large exhibitions of considerable artistic importance have been organized in the Republic. These have included the following: 'Socialist Byelorussia', 'In Praise of Work' and 'Byelorussian Graphic Art and Artistic Glassware'. There were, in addition, exhibitions to celebrate the thirtieth anniversary of the liberation of the Byelorussian SSR and the thirtieth anniversary of the victory over fascist Germany. The workers of the Republic also saw the exhibition 'Itinerant Russian Painters' with pictures from the museums of the USSR; the exhibition of Western European art, with items from the Dresden Museum; the exhibition of works of art from Poland; the exhibition of Western European and American art, with items from the museums of the United States of America; the exhibition of the graphic and folk art of Mexico; and exhibitions of works by painters from India and other countries. The Byelorussian Museum of Fine Arts has organized more than fifty exhibitions, attracting over 700,000 visitors. Travelling exhibitions have visited over 200 places in the Republic and were seen by some 150,00 people.

Protection of historical and cultural monuments

In the development of the culture of each of the fraternal peoples of the Soviet Union, importance is attached to the enhancement of the spiritual heritage handed down by preceding generations, which takes the form of all kinds of traditional and professional art. The finest traditions of this art and the noblest expressions of the people's creative genius are an inspiration to writers, painters and composers, giving them new strength to develop national and folk arts on socialist realism lines, and to combat the doctrines of formalist, abstract, cosmopolitan and other types of art.

In connection with cultural development, great importance is attached to the protection of all kinds of cultural monuments, architecture, sculpture, painting and history, and to the protection of important sites. As early as 30 January 1919, the provisional government of the workers and peasants of the Byelorussian SSR promulgated a decree 'on the need to hand over to the Commissariat for Education all objects of scientific and artistic value located in private properties and establishments of various kinds, to draw up a list of these objects and to arrange for their protection and collection'.

By about 1920, more than 550 ancient manorial properties had accordingly been listed in the Byelorussian SSR, and thousands of works of art.

In 1923, the Government of the Byelorussian SSR examined the question afresh and promulgated a decree 'on the listing and protection of monuments of history, art, everyday life and nature located in the territory of the Byelorussian SSR'. On 5 July 1925, the Government of the Republic ratified the first list of these monuments.

Since 1967, the protection of monuments located in the territory of the Byelorussian SSR has been the responsibility of the Ministry of Culture.

The law of the Byelorussian SSR 'Preservation and Utilization of Monuments of History and Culture' came into force on 1 November 1978.

The new law formulates the principles and aims of the preservation and utilization of historical and cultural monuments and defines the tasks of Soviet legislation in this field. It is directed at preserving the historical and cultural monuments in the Byelorussian SSR for present and future generations, at creating more favourable conditions for their scientific study and at effective utilization of them for aesthetic and moral education.

The basic feature of the new law is that it confirms once again the immutable fact that historical and cultural monuments are the true property of the people, and their preservation is declared to be a matter of great State and public concern.

According to the law, the State administration for protecting historical monuments is vested in the Council of Ministers of the Byelorussian SSR, executive committees of the local Soviets of People's Deputies and in specially authorized State bodies.

The law also provides for wide participation of public organizations, trade unions, youth organizations, scientific societies, creative unions and citizens in measures aimed at the protection, utilization, registration and restoration of monuments and dissemination of information about them.

The law attaches great importance to the activities of the Byelorussian Volunteer Society for the Protection of Historical and Cultural Monuments which has about 2 million members.

One of the most important provisions of the law states that money collected from the utilization of monuments is to be spent only on their restoration, repair and preservation.

According to the law, the export of historical and cultural property from the territory of the USSR is prohibited.

With a view to promoting international cultural exchange, a temporary transfer of property from the USSR is permitted.

There are in the Byelorussian SSR a number of important architectural monuments dating from ancient times. These include the Cathedral of Saint Sophia (built in the eleventh century and reconstructed in the eighteenth), the Church of the Saviour and Saint Ephrossinia (twelfth century) at Polotsk, and the Church of Saint Boris and Saint Gleb (twelfth century) at Grodno.

From the second half of the eighteenth century, both the purpose and the style of architecture changed considerably. The need to defend the land against foreign invaders led to the construction of fortified buildings like watch-towers, castles, etc. The most important of this type are the castles at Novogrudok and Lida, the tower at Kamenetsk (Belaja Vezha), the fortified churches of Synkovichi, Malomozejhkov and Suprasl, and the fortified palace at Mir.

Byelorussian architecture of the seventeenth and the first half of the eighteenth century is of an original baroque style. The eighteenth and nineteenth centuries have bequeathed to us some unique wooden buildings, the work of local builders from among the people. Protection and restoration of architectural monuments of artistic value form an integral feature of the cultural policy of the republic.

During their temporary occupation of the republic, Hitler's troops inflicted untold damage. They destroyed almost all the important monuments; 30 per cent of the architectural monuments were completely demolished, and more than 50 per cent seriously damaged.

After the victory, majestic memorials were set up, immortalizing the exploits of the people. These include the Khatyn memorial, perpetuating the memory of the inhabitants of the village of this name, and of 186 other Byelorussian villages, who were burned alive by the fascists;

the architectural and sculptural monument of the Hero-fortress of Brest, erected to the memory of all those who defended this town so heroically in 1941; the Mound of Glory near Minsk, built in honour of the Soviet army which liberated the Byelorussian SSR from the Hitlerite invaders in 1944; the Breakthrough memorial in the district of Uchachi; and the monument to the Soviet Patriot-Mother at Zhodino. The builders of the Khatyn memorial were awarded the Lenin prize, and those of the Mound of Glory, the Byelorussian SSR State prize.

Outstanding architectural achievements completed in the capital in the 1960s and 1970s include the Byelorussian State University, the Sports Palace, the Pavilion for the Exhibition of the Byelorussian Economic Achievements, the Jubilejnaja Hotel, the Minsk Palace of Arts and the House of Writers.

Measures for the protection of Byelorussian historical and cultural monuments go hand in hand with their utilization for the ideological and moral education of the people. It has become a tradition for young people to visit important places connected with the revolution, the war and labour, and to go on trips 'from monument to monument' and 'from obelisk to obelisk'. Special weeks are organized to commemorate the country's heroes. Over 19 million people have visited the Khatyn memorial, the Brest Hero-fortress, the Mound of Glory and other monuments since their inauguration.

Radio, television, cinema

In addition to the traditional channels for the spread of culture such as museums, theatres, concert halls and libraries, the cultural information and communication media like radio, television and the cinema are constantly developing.

The first radio stations started broadcasting in Minsk and Gomel in 1925. Since that time, work has proceeded uninterruptedly on the manufacture of increasingly powerful transmitters, construction of studios, and the introduction of new sound-recording techniques. The first radio relay station, set up in Minsk in 1927, was originally used for group reception in clubs, parks and 'red corners'. In 1931, a transmitter was opened near Minsk which broadcast the programmes of the Byelorussian radio service all over the Republic. Before the Great Patriotic War, the factory at Minsk, which was the first radio factory in the Byelorussian SSR, began to produce large quantities of receivers. Broadcasting was to become one of the main channels for informing the public and educating them politically and culturally.

During the temporary occupation of the Republic by the Nazis, the radio gave support to the unconquered Byelorussian people in their struggle for freedom and independence. The 'Soviet Byelorussia' station, whose programmes were heard throughout the Republic, was set up in the autumn of 1941. The radio service of the partisan units and brigades provided the population with impartial news about the progress of hostilities, international events and life in the Soviet Union. Immediately after the liberation of Gomel, in November 1943, a mobile radio transmitter began regular transmissions of the programmes of Radio Byelorussia.

At present, Byelorussian listeners can tune in to three All Union and two Republican programmes, in addition to which each region has a programme of its own.

Television, which constitutes the most effective channel for cultural information and communication, exercises an enormous influence on the attitudes of the Soviet people. The first Byelorussian television centre was opened in Minsk in 1955; since then other stations have come into service.

The television transmission network is based on the economic and rational principle of a system of relay stations and cable circuits. The Byelorussian television centre transmits its programmes on three channels. In addition, Byelorussian viewers can watch the programmes of local studios and those of the central television service. New television stations and telecommunications lines are continuing to be built. Since 1967, the main television stations of the Republic have been transmitting the colour programmes of the All Union television system of the USSR and, in 1974, the Minsk station began to transmit the colour programmes of Byelorussian television.

At the present time, every Byelorussian family possesses its own radio and television sets.

The production of films in the Republic began in the 1920s, after the Government of the Byelorussian SSR had decided to set up the Belgoskino studios. The first news-reels were made in 1925. In 1926, Y. Tarich produced the first feature film, *The Story of the Forest*. In 1930, a collection of sound films was made, consisting of documentaries and cartoons. The first talking film, *Into the Fight*, was produced in 1932. The three 'Belarusfilm' studios now shoot more than forty full-length films a year, including documentaries and popular science films, for both cinema and television.

The best Belarusfilm productions rank among the most outstanding films of the multinational Soviet cinema. These have included *Born in the Flames, July the Eleventh, Born Twice, Konstantin Zaslonov, The Red Leaves, The Clock Stopped at Midnight, She is Seeking Her Daddy, Moscow-Genoa, Alpine Ballad, The Flames, Ivan Makarovich, The Time of Her Sons, Sketches for a Portrait, The Eagle's Source, Put to Death in 1941, The X Bird, The Gold Hunt, The Woman From a Destroyed Village, Twenty Years Afterwards or the Hopes and Fears of Class 10A.*

There are about 7,000 cinemas in the Republic and a large number of fixed and mobile projection units.

International cultural relations

Cultural relations with foreign countries are maintained by both voluntary and State organizations. The Ministry of Culture of the Byelorussian SSR and the Byelorussian Society for Friendship and Cultural Relations with Foreign Countries, founded in 1926, do important work in this field. At present, this society comprises 11 republican sections, 8 regional sections, 28 town and district sections, and 132 local sections. With the support of all groups of the population, the society maintains friendly contacts with over 300 voluntary and cultural organizations, and with thousands of eminent personalities and representatives of science and culture in dozens of foreign countries.

Each year, delegates from voluntary organizations representing writers, artists and cultural workers, visit a large number of countries in the world. Groups of professionals and amateurs, eminent artists, creative workers and tourists go abroad to take part in events devoted to Byelorussian art, to participate in festivals and competitions, and to study the work of cultural and art establishments in foreign countries. The Republic's leading artistic personalities performed at the solemn evening gathering held at Unesco Headquarters in Paris to mark the ninetieth anniversary of the birth of the national poets of the Byelorussian SSR, Y. Kupala and Y. Kolas. They also performed in the Czechoslovak Socialist Republic, the German Democratic Republic, France, the United Kingdom, Sweden and various other countries. The Byelorussian Dance Company toured Cuba, the Democratic People's Republic of Korea and Latin America. The Byelorussian Opera and Ballet Company went to Hungary to take part in the 'Szeged Games', and also toured Poland. The I. Zhinovich National Orchestra took part in the Festival of Peace and Friendship in Czechoslovakia, and has given concerts in Austria. The Y. Kupala Academic Theatre and the Pesnjary Vocal and Instrumental Troupe took part in the festival of Soviet culture held in Switzerland.

In 1976, 300 or so representatives of Byelorussian culture visited some thirty countries of the world.

Amateur groups also pay visits to foreign countries. For example, the People's Song and Dance Troupe from the Cultural Centre at Molodechno (Minsk region) took part in the International Folklore Festival at Burgos. The Radost Dance Troupe from the Brest Cultural Centre represented Byelorussian amateur art at the International Folk-art Festival held in France and at the Festival of Soviet Culture in Italy. There was an exhibition in Bulgaria of the work of the corresponding member of the USSR Academy of Fine Arts, Mikhail Savitski, a national painter of the Byelorussian SSR. Exhibitions of the work of M. Savitski and V. Gromyko were held in the German Democratic Republic, and in India there was an exhibition of the works of Y. Poplavski who was awarded the Jawaharlal Nehru international prize. During 1976 alone, exhibitions of the work of Byelorussian painters were held in Austria, Denmark and the Federal Republic of Germany. Over the past few years, many painters have made study trips abroad.

The Byelarusfilm studios have made co-productions with film workers from Czechoslovakia and Bulgaria (Tomorrow Will Be Too Late, *Bratushka, The Little Sergeant,* etc.). Byelorussian representatives of various forms of art have been awarded a number of prizes and decorations at international competitions, exhibitions and festivals. At the tenth Youth and Student Festival in Berlin, the political song prize was awarded to the Pesnjary Vocal and Instrumental Troupe. The first violin of the Minsk Chamber Music Orchestra, A. Kramarov, was awarded first prize at the twentieth Paganini International Violin Competition in Italy. At the Prague Spring International Piano Competition in Czechoslovakia, the prize winner was I. Olovnikov, laureate of the Byelorussian State Academy of Music. A Kuzmine received a special mention.

Many well-known artistic troupes and performers from various countries of the world visit the Byelorussian SSR every year. Those who have come to the Byelorussian SSR in recent years include the Vienna Symphony Orchestra, the Mazowsze Folk Song and Dance Company, the Los Angeles Choir, the National Ensemble, Dances of Venezuela, the Bucharest Madrigal Choir, the Coliseum Musicum Choir from Yugoslavia, the Bulgarian Radio and Television Symphony Orchestras, the Lodz Philharmonic, the Polish Army Orchestra, the Belgrade Radio and Television Choir, and the Komische Oper ballets from the German Democratic Republic.

In 1976, over a thousand artists from more than twenty countries of the world visited the Byelorussian SSR.

Every year, a large number of events devoted to the literature and arts of foreign countries are organized in the Byelorussian SSR.

Cultural activities and sports

A vast network of cultural and sports establishments exists in the Byelorussian SSR, where the workers are able not only to rest and improve their health, but also to deepen their general culture, improve their education and satisfy their intellectual, spiritual and artistic ambitions.

Libraries

Public and specialist libraries now form an integral part of the everyday, social and working lives of our people. In the Byelorussian SSR there are some 20,000 libraries of all types possessing stocks of about 170 million volumes. Every year the number of readers increases, the choice of reading matter grows wider, and the books are put to more efficient use. By investigating readers' wants and needs in depth, libraries are continually improving the services they offer the public.

The main scientific centre for Byelorussian libraries is the Lenin State Library. In all the towns and regional centres of the Republic there are libraries where readers can find the books they want, or where they can order them through the interlibrary loan service. Readers in remote villages are served by mobile libraries or lending centres.

Libraries are playing a greater and greater part in the intellectual developement of workers. In accordance with the decree of the Central Committee of the CPSU on 'enlarging the contribution of libraries to the communist education of the workers and to scientific and technical progress', steps are being taken all over the Soviet Union, including the Byelorussian SSR, to centralize the work of the public libraries by setting up a network of town and district libraries with common stocks centrally distributed and selected. Libraries encourage reading in a variety of ways including exhibitions, public discussions about books and the distribution of information about new books. They also organize literary and musical evenings and games of various kinds such as literary charades.

Public and specialist libraries make every effort to promote scientific and technological progress, and contribute to the social and cultural changes occurring in the Soviet Union.

Clubs

Originally established at the time of the Great October Revolution to act as new political and social centres, clubs have now become part of the life of our people. There are over 6,400 clubs in the Byelorussian SSR today and these, in conjunction with the cultural centres, do extremely important political work among the general public. These activities most commonly take the form of evenings devoted to certain themes, conferences, political discussions, competitions, festivals, etc.

People's cultural university courses are generally held in the clubs and cultural centres and are playing an increasingly important part in the ideological and aesthetic education of the workers, introducing workers to the various forms of culture and art and encouraging them to embark on creative activities. The instruction which is given covers the theoretical and practical problems of the development of culture, the history of literature and art, both indigenous and foreign, and the work of eminent composers, writers, painters, stage producers and film directors. At these people's universities, students acquire a sound knowledge of major Soviet and foreign artistic achievement and of the main lines of development of various forms of art.

In 1976, the Republic possessed 240 people's cultural universities with 55 branches, attended by approximately 50,000 people.

As the cultural universities grow more numerous, they are also becoming more differentiated, with universities specializing in one form of art predominating over those providing education of a general type.

Amateur art and popular creative activities

Amateur art constitutes one form of art education for the general public. There are over 36,000 amateur artistic groups in the Byelorussian SSR devoted to the theatre, music, choreography, applied art and other forms of creative activity. This amateur social activity engaged in by people in different walks of life and of different ages and educational levels, brings workers to adopt a creative attitude towards work and refines their taste.

Since the mid-1930s, amateur art festivals and competitions have been held in the Byelorussian SSR as well as exhibitions of the work of people's artists and amateurs. In 1937, republican and regional centres for popular artistic activities were created to provide professional and methodological guidance in the field of amateur art. 1968 saw the creation of the trade-union amateur art activities centre.

The most popular forms of amateur artistic activities are music and singing. Firms and collective farms often have several choirs, orchestras and instrumental and vocal ensembles. The best known are the choirs of the Minsk automobile and tractor works, the folk-instrument ensembles of the Railwaymen's Cultural Centre at Gomel, the Byelorussian State University and the Republic Trade Union Cultural Centre, the Radost Choreographic Ensemble at Brest, the Chorale of the Mogilev Cultural Centre, the Kolos Popular Choreographic Ensemble at the Vitebsk Cultural Centre, the People's Dramatic Theatre at Slonim, and the Popular Song and Dance Troupe of the Novogrudok District Cultural Centre.

To encourage mass amateur artistic activities, all kinds of competitions, festivals and exhibitions are regularly organized. The first national festival of amateur art was held from 1975 to 1977 with more than 600,000 amateur artists in the Byelorussian SSR taking part.

Traditional folk art such as poetry and music, decorative art, applied art, visual art, choreography, drama and other forms of artistic activity is flourishing at the present time.

Traditional songs are made widely known through radio, television and the cinema. A study of Byelorussian folk music shows that, thanks to the 'artistic schools' for training in folk art, which have developed over the centuries, the Republic possesses a very rich heritage of folk music.

The applied folk arts like pottery, wood-carving, weaving and basket-making, continue to develop, and businesses specializing in the production of art-ware have recently been set up. There are more than 6,000 folk artists working in this field in the Byelorussian SSR.

The best work of amateur artists is on display in the Soviet Byelorussia pavilion of the Exhibition of the Economic Achievements of the USSR. It has also been exhibited in Bulgaria, the German Democratic Republic, Mongolia, Poland, France, Finland, the United Kingdom, Belgium, Switzerland, Italy, the United States, Cuba, Canada and a number of other countries.

P. M. Masherov, alternate member of the Politburo of the Central Committee of the CPSU and First Secretary of the Central Committee of the Communist Party of the Byelorussian SSR, has stated:

We are particularly concerned to ensure the correct development of amateur art, which is not only a factor for the rational organization of workers' leisure time but also a perennial source of popular talent to swell our artistic culture. In view of the increase of popular activity in this field and the rise in the standard of amateur group work during the past few years, it is essential to take more active measures to encourage amateur art to use and develop the rich traditions of folk art. [1]

The research institutes, unions of creative workers and cultural establishments of the Republic are thus all contributing greatly to the development of the best folk traditions and other forms of folk art.

In the Byelorussian SSR, amateur art maintains close links with professional and popular art, a collaboration which works to the advantage of all. Professionals give advice to amateur groups, help gifted young people to develop their skills in specialist teaching establishments and pick out talented amateurs in their communities. At the same time, amateur artistic activities help professional artists to understand people's ambitions, interests and ideals, which they are then able to reflect more faithfully in their own works. Some professional organizations and artists sponsor amateur groups. For instance, the Y. Kupala Academic Theatre sponsors the artistic activities of amateurs of the Y. Kupala State Farm (district of Molodechno). People's universities of dramatic art have been established in conjunction with the Vitebsk and Grodno dramatic theatres. The regional theatres, creative workers' unions and artistic organizations have staff to organize relations with amateur artists. The repertoire of both professional and amateur groups reflects the close links existing between them.

Physical culture and sport

In the Byelorussian SSR, the Communist Party and the government pay constant attention to physical education and sport. Sports activities in the Republic are organized by the Committee of Physical Culture and Sport attached to the Council of Ministers.

In the Byelorussian SSR, the physical education system for the people is planned on a scientific basis. The first stage begins in preschool establishments, where the children are introduced to gymnastics and sports. Physical culture lessons are given in the general and specialized secondary schools. The Republic has 8 higher sports training schools and over 300 sports schools for children and adolescents. In higher educational establishments, physical culture and sports are compulsory. Several business and establishments in the Republic have introduced the practice of exercises during working hours.

The physical culture groups set up in businesses, building sites, State and collective farms, offices and educational establishments form the basis of the sports system. These groups now number over 10,500. Physical culture and sport are practised regularly by over 2 million people.

1. *Communist of Byelorussia*, 1971, No. 3, p. 31.

Cultural activities and sports

Physical culture groups are affiliated to voluntary sports associations such as Dynamo, Burevestnik, Vodnik, and Krasnoe Znamja.

The physical education system of the Republic employs over 12,000 teachers and coaches. The best of these are awarded the title 'Honoured Worker (or Coach) of the Byelorussian SSR'. Physical education and sports teachers are trained at the Byelorussian Institute of Physical Culture and Sports and in the physical culture and sports faculties of the University of Gomel, the Institute of Education at Brest, the Republican Training School and the physical education colleges at Vitebsk and Grodno.

It has been possible to put plans for the development of physical culture into effect thanks to the creation and regular expansion of modern sports facilities. There are at present in the Byelorussian SSR nearly 100 stadiums, about 60 swimming pools, over 2,500 gymnasiums and about 40,000 volleyball courts. The most important sports facilities in the Republic are the Dynamo Stadium in Minsk, the Minsk Sports Palace, the Republican Nautical Stadium, and the Raubichi Sports Complex.

Since 1952, sportsmen from the Byelorussian SSR have formed part of the USSR national teams competing in the Olympic Games and world championships.

Minsk has been the site of several international Graeco-Roman and free-style wrestling contests and competitions in gymnastics, swimming, boxing, the biathlon, etc. A number of Byelorussians have been Olympic and world champions and have won prizes in various international competitions.

Planning and financing of educational, scientific and cultural activities

The purpose of the planning and financing of the cultural development of the Byelorussian SSR is to develop public education, science and culture, to raise the general standard of education, to improve the quality of personnel training and to meet the cultural needs of all members of society.

Educational and cultural activities are financed from the national budget of the Byelorussian SSR under the heading of social and cultural measures. The funds allocated for these activities come under different items of the budget such as education, science, culture, public health, physical culture, or social security. The budget estimate for culture in 1977 was 1,946.3 million roubles, an increase of 5.5 per cent on the figure for 1976.

The number of pre-school establishments is increasing constantly. It was hoped that in 1977, crèches and kindergartens would be able to admit 5.5 per cent more children than in previous years, and the State was to allocate 81.6 million roubles for the upkeep of these establishments.

In 1977 also, 316,4 million roubles were to be earmarked for the running and extension of general educational schools and the improvement of their material and technical facilities.

There was also to be an increase in the number of schools adopting the 'prolonged school day' system (for pupils in grades 1 to 8); and there was to be more boarding schools, payment for which would be based on parents' salaries. Many families pay reduced fees or are exempt from fees altogether.

The national budget of the Byelorussian SSR finances a large network of cultural establishments coming under the Ministry of Culture like urban and rural clubs, cultural centres, museums and so on. When planning the development of the network of cultural establishments, theatres, musical institutions, newspaper offices, cinemas, and radio and

47

television stations, attention is paid to their even distribution over the territory of the Republic so as to ensure that people living in rural areas are served as well as those elsewhere.

Scientific and technological progress and the development of the Soviet economy call for highly qualified specialists. In 1977, it was planned to allocate 230.6 million roubles to the training of high-level Byelorussian personnel—6 per cent more than in 1976.

Personnel of this level are trained in vocational, specialist secondary, and higher educational establishments.

The training of middle and higher level specialists is planned by the ministries and administrative departments in charge of educational establishments, and the aim is to provide all the specialists needed in every branch of the economy. To cater for persons undergoing part-time specialist training while still at work, certain practical measures have been taken to improve the effectiveness of the various kinds of instruction which they receive.

Higher and specialist secondary education establishments are financed from the national budget of the Byelorussian SSR. In 1977, expenditure on improvements to the equipment of these establishments, on increasing the number of students attending them and on the introduction of new teaching techniques was to increase to 133.8 million roubles—4 per cent more than in 1976. Teachers' salaries are calculated according to the posts they hold, their university degrees (doctor, master (candidate) of science) and their length of service (under five years, from five to ten years, more than ten years). Funds for education and for the purchase of books for libraries vary according to the type of teaching (day, evening or correspondence courses). Funds for practical study courses are calculated according to the number of students and the duration of the course. The budgets of higher educational establishments include special funds for research.

The budget for day courses of higher educational establishments covers the cost of study grants. Plans also provide for grants for students attending post-graduate courses at higher educational establishments.

Funds for specialized secondary education establishments cover the cost of training middle-level specialists for the various branches of the national economy and culture. Plans for the financing of these establishments include the cost of grants and practical work by students.

The running costs for vocational training schools were expected to be 92.1 million roubles in 1977—8 per cent more than in 1976.

Appropriate material and financial resources are allocated for the development of science. Plans for technical progress and the development of the national economy are drawn up on the basis of scientific forecasts worked out by the State Planning Committee, the Academy of Sciences, the State Building Committee and the appropriate ministries and administrative departments of the Byelorussians SSR.

Research establishments are financed mainly from the national budget of the Republic and by the revenue derived from the work done under contract by these establishments. The national budget of the Republic also bears the bulk of the costs of research on the main scientific and technical problems and the natural sciences, and of the majority of research into the development of the various branches of the economy. In 1977, budgetary expenditure on this time was expected to be 47.6 million roubles.

In addition to the research work carried out by specialized scientific centres, important research is also done by higher education establishments with finance from several different sources, the chief of which are as follows: the national budget; special subsidies from the appropriate ministries and administrative departments; revenue from work done under contract; revenue from the workshops of teaching establishments, etc.

The upkeep of the laboratories of higher educational establishments carrying out fundamental scientific research is also financed from the State budget.

In addition to covering the salaries of researchers, funds for research work cover the costs of providing training and further training for scientists. There are annual and long-term plans for the training of scientists and teachers through post-graduate courses and through the 'study leave' granted to researchers preparing their theses.

The sum set aside in the national budget of the Byelorussian SSR for theatres, cultural centres, libraries, the cinema, television, radio and the periodical press was expected to be 36.2 million roubles in 1977.

Theatres and entertainment halls which do not manage to cover their expenses receive State subsidies, the size of which depends on the type of production staged and the financial situation of the establishment in question.

Plans for the development of the cinema provide for extending the network of projection units and for increasing film production. In planning the extension of the cinema network, attention is paid to the number of cinemas existing in towns and in the countryside, to the need to improve the equipment of existing projection and to review the practical arrangements for hiring films.

Plans for the number of films to be made are based on the creative and production capacity of the studios, and the probable rate of production during the year. Efforts are made to accelerate production and reduce costs.

To increase the number of publications, the most important step is to improve the material and cultural level and the education of the people and give them more leisure time which will, in turn, lead to an ever-increasing demand for certain books. What is published depends on the orders placed by the book trade.

49

Conclusion

The historic revolutionary achievements of the Soviet people, their successes in building the communist society and their victories on the difficult path followed by the country of the Soviets for over sixty years represent a direct continuation of the Great October Revolution, and the practical application of the ideas of that outstanding man Lenin.

The Soviet people, through their self-sacrificing labours, have succeeded in building an advanced socialist society.

Historical experience has shown that socialism has created unprecedented conditions for the social, economic and spiritual development of society, and has greatly accelerated the spiritual development of the Soviet State and the whole of the Soviet people. The creation of a historically new kind of community, the Soviet people, has gone hand in hand with the development of a special form of culture embodying the main features of this community. The culture of the people of the Soviet Union, including the people of the Byelorussian SSR, has developed on the basis of the unity of economic, social and spiritual life, Marxist-Leninist ideology and communist ideals. This culture is the culture of the whole people, and it brings to the fore the noble ideals of internationalism, friendship between peoples and revolutionary humanism. It is the mainspring of social progress, the harmonious development of man and his moral and intellectual development.

The advanced socialist society set up in the country of the Soviets is distinguished by the richness of intellectual life, the flowering of science and art, the high level of social consciousness and education of the working population. Advanced socialism is characterized by the rapid intellectualization of labour due to the influence of the scientific and technological revolution, by the constant improvement of the cultural level of the people, the elimination of differences between the cultural levels of town and countryside and the flowering of a single multinational culture. 'Today', as the Secretary-General of the Central Committee of the CPSU and Chairman of the Presidium of the Supreme Soviet of the USSR, L. I. Brezhnev, has said, 'we are entitled to say that our culture is socialist in substance and in the main lines of its development, that it has a variety of national forms, and that it is international in spirit and nature. It is an organic combination of the spiritual values created by all the peoples.'[1]

Culture, in a socialist society, does not develop at random, but pursues a specific aim. The ideological and spiritual progress of society, including that of communist instruction and education and the development of culture and the arts, is directed by the Communist Party on the basis of a knowledge of the objective laws of social development. The Party does everything to ensure that cultural progress serves to promote the well-being of society and of every individual.

At its XXVth Congress, the CPSU laid down, in close co-ordination with the main objectives of economic, social and political development, far-reaching plans for the continuous progress of socialist culture which, at the stage of advanced socialism, is to embrace all spheres of the activity of society and the life of man.

The increasingly important role of socialist culture is an important factor for the development of the whole of the life of society. It helps workers to develop more harmoniously, to give expression to their creative capacities, to increase their social requirements and to use their creative energy for the implementation of the mighty programme for the building of communism, drawn up by the XXVth Congress of the Communist Party of the Soviet Union.

1. Brezhnev, op. cit, p. 59-60.

Titles in this series:

The serial numbering of titles in this series, the presentation of which has been modified, was discontinued with the volume *Cultural policy in Italy*